I0164052

Christ Our Advocate

to include:

Christ *the* Husband *of the* Church

All Things *for* Good *to*
Those *that* Love God

Charles G. Finney

MB

Copyright © 2018 Merchant Books

ISBN 978-1-60386-764-1

DIGITALIZED BY
WATCHMAKER PUBLISHING
ALL RIGHTS RESERVED

Christ Our Advocate

And if any man sin we have an Advocate with the Father, Jesus Christ, the righteous. And he is the propitiation for our sins; and not for ours only, but also for the sins of the whole world.[1]

The Bible abounds with governmental analogies. These are designed for our instruction; but if we receive instruction from them, it is because there is a real analogy in many points between the government of God and human governments.

I propose to inquire,

I. What is an advocate?

What is the idea of an advocate when the term is used to express a governmental office or relation?

An advocate is one who pleads the cause of another; who represents another, and acts in his name; one who uses his influence in behalf of another by his request.

II. Purposes for which an advocate may he employed.

1. To secure justice, in case any question involving justice is to be tried.

2. To defend the accused. If one has been accused of committing a crime, an advocate may be employed to conduct his trial on his behalf; to defend him against the charge, and prevent his conviction if possible.

3. An advocate may be employed to secure a pardon, when a criminal has been justly condemned, and is under sentence. That is, an advocate may be employed either to secure justice for his client, or to obtain mercy for him, in case he is condemned; may be employed either to prevent his conviction, or when convicted, may be employed in setting aside the execution of the law upon the criminal.

---

[1] *1 John ii. 1, 2*

III. The sense in which Christ is the advocate of sinners.

He is employed to plead the cause of sinners, not at the bar of justice; not to defend them against the charge of sin, because the question of their guilt is already settled. The Bible represents them as condemned already; and such is the fact, as every sinner knows. Every sinner in the world knows that he has sinned, and that consequently he must be condemned by the law of God. This office, then, is exercised by Christ in respect to sinners; not at the bar of justice, but at the throne of grace, at the footstool of sovereign mercy. He is employed, not to prevent the conviction of the sinner, but to prevent his execution; not to prevent his being condemned, but being already condemned, to prevent his being damned.

IV. What is implied in His being the Advocate of sinners.

1. His being employed at a throne of grace and not at the bar of justice, to plead for sinners, as such, and not for those who are merely charged with sin, but the charge not established. This implies that the guilt of the sinner is already ascertained, the verdict of guilty given, the sentence of the law pronounced, and that the sinner awaits his execution.

2. His being appointed by God as the Advocate of sinners implies a merciful disposition in God. If God had not been mercifully disposed towards sinners, no Advocate had been appointed, no question of forgiveness had been raised.

3. It implies also that the exercise of mercy on certain conditions is possible. Not only is God mercifully disposed, but to manifest this disposition in the actual pardon of sin is possible. Had not this been the case, no Advocate had been appointed.

4. It implies that there is hope, then, for the condemned. Sinners are prisoners; but in this world they are not yet prisoners of despair, but are prisoners of hope.

5. It implies that there is a governmental necessity for the interposition of an advocate; that the sinner's relations are such, and his character such, that he cannot be admitted to plead his own cause in his own name. He is condemned, he is no longer on trial. In this respect he is under sentence for a capital crime; consequently, he is an outlaw, and the government cannot recognize him as being capable of performing any legal act. His relations to the government forbid that in his own name, or

in his own person, he should appear before God. So far as his own personal influence with the government is concerned, he is as a dead man – he is civilly dead. Therefore, he must appear by his next friend, or by his advocate, if he is heard at all. He may not appear in his own name and in his own person but must appear by an advocate who is acceptable to the government.

V. The essential qualifications of an advocate under such circumstances.

1. He must be the uncompromising friend of the government. Observe, he appears to pray for mercy to be extended to the guilty party whom he represents. Of course, he must not himself be the enemy of the government of whom he asks so great a favor; but he should be known to be the devoted friend of the government whose mercy he prays may be extended to the guilty.

2. He must be the uncompromising friend of the dishonored law. The sinner has greatly dishonored, and by his conduct denounced, both the law and the Law-giver. By his uniform disobedience the sinner has proclaimed, in the most emphatic manner, that the law is not worthy of obedience, and that the Law-giver is a tyrant. Now the Advocate must be a friend to this law; he must not sell himself to the dishonor of the law nor consent to its dishonor. He must not reflect upon the law; for in this case he places the Law-giver in a position in which, if he should set aside the penalty and exercise mercy, he would consent to the dishonor of the law, and by a public act himself condemn the law. The Advocate seeks to dispense with the execution of the law; but he must not offer, as a reason, that the law is unreasonable and unjust. For in this case he renders it impossible for the Law-giver to set aside the execution without consenting to the assertion that the law is not good. In that case the Law-giver would condemn himself instead of the sinner. It is plain, then, that he must be the uncompromising friend of the law, or he can never secure the exercise of mercy without involving the Law-giver himself in the crime of dishonoring the law.

3. The Advocate must be righteous; that is, he must be clear of any complicity in the crime of the sinner. He must have no fellowship with his crime; there must be no charge or suspicion of guilt resting upon the Advocate. Unless he himself be clear of the crime of which the criminal

is accused, he is not the proper person to represent him before a throne of mercy.

4. He must be the compassionate friend of the sinner – not of his sins, but of the sinner himself. This distinction is very plain. Everyone knows that a parent can be greatly opposed to the wickedness of his children, while he has great compassion for their person. He is not a true friend to the sinner who really sympathizes with his sins. I have several times heard sinners render as an excuse for not being Christians, that their friends were opposed to it. They have a great many dear friends who are opposed to their becoming Christians and obeying God. They desire them to live on in their sins. They do not want them to change and become holy, but desire them to remain in their worldly-mindedness and sinfulness. I tell such persons that those are their friends in the same sense that the devil is their friend.

And would they call the devil their good friend, their kind friend, because he sympathizes with their sins, and wishes them not to become Christians? Would you call a man your friend, who wished you to commit murder, or robbery, to tell a lie, or commit any crime? Suppose he should come and appeal to you, and because you are his friend should desire you to commit some great crime, would you regard that man as your friend?

No! No man is a true friend of a sinner, unless he is desirous that he should abandon his sins. If any person would have you continue in your sins, he is the adversary of your soul. Instead of being in any proper sense your friend, he is playing the devil's part to ruin you.

Now observe: Christ is the compassionate friend of sinners, a friend in the best and truest sense. He does not sympathize with your sins, but His heart is set upon saving you from your sins. I said He must be the compassionate friend of sinners; and His compassion must be stronger than death, or He will never meet the necessities of the case.

5. Another qualification must be, that He is able sufficiently to honor the law, which sinners by their transgression have dishonored. He seeks to avoid the execution of the dishonored law of God. The law having been dishonored by sin in the highest degree, must either be honored by its execution on the criminal, or the Law-giver must in some other way bear testimony in favor of the law, before He can justly dispense with the execution of its penalty. The law is not to be repealed; the law must not be dishonored. It is the law of God's nature, the unalterable law of His

government, the eternal law of heaven, the law for the government of moral agents in all worlds, and in all time, and to all eternity. Sinners have borne their most emphatic testimony against it, by pouring contempt upon it in utterly refusing to obey it. Now sin must not be treated lightly – this law must be honored.

God might pour a flash of glory over it by executing its penalty upon the whole race that have despised it. This would be the solemn testimony of God to sustain its authority and vindicate its claims. If our Advocate appears before God to ask for the remission of sin, that the penalty of this law may be set aside and not executed, the question immediately arises, but how shall the dishonor of this law be avoided? What shall compensate for the reckless and blasphemous contempt with which this law has been treated? How shall sin be forgiven without apparently making light of it?

It is plain that sin has placed the whole question in such a light that God's testimony must in some way be borne in a most emphatic manner against sin, and to sustain the authority of this dishonored law.

It behooves the Advocate of sinners to provide Himself with a plea that shall meet this difficulty. He must meet this necessity, if He would secure the setting aside of the penalty. He must be able to provide an adequate substitute for its execution. He must be able to do that which will as effectually bear testimony in favor of the law and against sin, as the execution of the law upon the criminal would do. In other words, He must be able to meet the demands of public justice.

6. He must be willing to volunteer a gratuitous service. He cannot be called upon in justice to volunteer a service or suffer for the sake of sinners. He may volunteer His service and it may be accepted; but if He does volunteer His service, He must be able and willing to endure whatever pain or sacrifice is necessary to meet the case.

If the law must be honored by obedience; if, "without the shedding of blood, there can be no remission;" if an emphatic governmental testimony must be borne against sin, and in honor of the law; if He must become the representative of sinners, offering Himself before the whole universe as a propitiation for sin, He must be willing to meet the case and make the sacrifice.

7. He must have a good plea. In other words, when He appears before the mercy-seat, He must be able to present such considerations as shall

really meet the necessities of the case, and render it safe, proper, honorable, glorious in God to forgive.

VI. What His plea in behalf of sinners is.

It should be remembered that the appeal is not to justice. Since the fall of man, God has plainly suspended the execution of strict justice upon our race. To us, as a matter of fact, He has set upon a throne of mercy. Mercy, and not justice, has been the rule of His administration, since men were involved in sin.

This is simple fact. Men do sin, and they are not cut off immediately and sent to hell. The execution of justice is suspended; and God is represented as seated upon a throne of grace, or upon a mercy-seat. It is here at a mercy-seat that Christ executes the office of Advocate for sinners.

2. Christ's plea for sinners cannot be that they are not guilty. They are guilty, and condemned. No question can be raised as it respects their guilt and their ill-desert; such questions are settled. It has often appeared strange to me that men overlook the fact that they are condemned already, and that no question respecting their guilt or desert of punishment can ever be raised.

3. Christ as our Advocate cannot, and need not, plead a justification. A plea of justification admits the fact charged; but asserts that under the circumstances the accused had a right to do as he did. This plea Christ can never make. This is entirely out of place, the case having been already tried, and sentence passed.

4. He may not plead what will reflect, in any wise, upon the law. He cannot plead that the law was too strict in its precept, or too severe in its penalty; for in that case he would not really plead for mercy, but for justice. He would plead in that case that no injustice might be done the criminal. For if he intimates that the law is not just, then the sinner does not deserve the punishment; hence it would be unjust to punish him, and his plea would amount to this, that the sinner be not punished, because he does not deserve it. But if this plea should be allowed to prevail, it would be a public acknowledgment on the part of God that His law was unjust. But this may never be.

5. He may not plead anything that shall reflect upon the administration of the Law-giver. Should he plead that men had been

hardly treated by the Law-giver, either in their creation, or by His providential arrangements, or by suffering them to be so tempted – or if, in any wise, he brings forward a plea that reflects upon the Law-giver, in creation, or in the administration of His government, the Law-giver cannot listen to his plea, and forgive the sinner, without condemning Himself. In that case, instead of insisting that the sinner should repent, virtually the Law-giver would be called upon Himself to repent.

6. He may not plead any excuse whatever for the sinner in mitigation of his guilt, or in extenuation of his conduct. For if he does, and the Law-giver should forgive in answer to such a plea, He would confess that He had been wrong, and that the sinner did not deserve the sentence that had been pronounced against him.

He must not plead that the sinner does not deserve the damnation of hell; for, should he urge this plea, it would virtually accuse the justice of God, and would be equivalent to begging that the sinner might not be sent unjustly to hell. This would not be a proper plea for mercy, but rather an issue with justice. It would be asking that the sinner might not be sent to hell, not because of the mercy of God, but because the justice of God forbids it. This will never be.

7. He cannot plead as our Advocate that He has paid our debt, in such a sense that He can demand our discharge on the ground of justice. He has not paid our debt in such a sense that we do not still owe it. He has not atoned for our sins in such a sense that we might not still be justly punished for them. Indeed, such a thing is impossible and absurd. One being cannot suffer for another in such a sense as to remove the guilt of that other. He may suffer for another's guilt in such a sense that it will be safe to forgive the sinner, for whom the suffering has been endured; but the suffering of the substitute can never, in the least degree, diminish the intrinsic guilt of the criminal. Our Advocate may urge that He has borne such suffering for us to honor the law that we had dishonored, that now it is safe to extend mercy to us; but He never can demand our discharge on the ground that we do not deserve to be punished. The fact of our intrinsic guilt remains and must forever remain; and our forgiveness is just as much an act of sovereign mercy, as if Christ had never died for us.

8. But Christ may plead His sin-offering to sanction the law, as fulfilling a condition, upon which we may be forgiven.

This offering is not to be regarded as the ground upon which justice demands our forgiveness. The appeal of our Advocate is not to this offering as payment in such a sense that now in justice He can demand that we shall be set free. No. As I said before, it is simply the fulfilling of a condition, upon which it is safe for the mercy of God to arrest and set aside the execution of the law, in the case of the penitent sinner.

Some theologians appear to me to have been unable to see this distinction. They insist upon it that the atonement of Christ is the ground of our forgiveness. They seem to assume that He literally bore the penalty for us in such a sense that Christ now no longer appeals to mercy but demands justice for us. To be consistent they must maintain that Christ does not plead at a mercy-seat for us, but having paid our debt, appears before a throne of justice, and demands our discharge.

I cannot accept this view. I insist that His offering could not touch the question of our intrinsic desert of damnation. His appeal is to the infinite mercy of God, to His loving disposition to pardon; and He points to His atonement, not as demanding our release, but as fulfilling a condition upon which our release is honorable to God. His obedience to the law and the shedding of His blood He may plead as a substitute for the execution of the law upon us – in short, He may plead the whole of His work as God-man and Mediator. Thus, He may give us the full benefit of what He has done to sustain the authority of law and to vindicate the character of the Law-giver, as fulfilling conditions that have rendered it possible for God to be just and still justify the penitent sinner.

9. But the plea is directed to the merciful disposition of God. He may point to the promise made to him in Isaiah, chap. 52d, from v. 13 to the end, and chap. 53, vs. 1, 2: "Behold, my servant shall deal prudently, he shall be exalted and extolled, and be very high.

"As many were astonished at thee; (his visage was so marred more than any man, and his form more than the sons of men:)

"So shall he sprinkle many nations; the kings shall shut their mouths at him: for that which had not been told them shall they see; and that which they had not heard shall they consider.

"Who hath believed our report? and to whom is the arm of the Lord revealed?

"For he shall grow up before him as a tender plant, and as a root out of a dry ground: he hath no form nor comeliness; and when we shall see him, there is no beauty that we should desire him."

10. He may plead also that He becomes our surety, that He undertakes for us, that He is our wisdom, and righteousness, and sanctification, and redemption; and point to His official relations. His infinite fullness, willingness, and ability to restore us to obedience, and to fit us for the service, the employments, and enjoyments of heaven. It is said that He is made the surety of a better covenant than the legal one; and a covenant founded upon better promises.

11. He may urge as a reason for our pardon the great pleasure it will afford to God, to set aside the execution of the law. "Mercy rejoiceth against judgment." Judgment is His strange work; but He delighteth in mercy.

It is said of Victoria that when her prime minister presented a pardon, and asked her if she would sign a pardon in the case of some individual who was sentenced to death, she seized the pen, and said, "Yes! with all my heart!" Could such an appeal be made to a woman's heart, think you, without its leaping for joy to be placed in a position in which it could save the life of a fellow-being?

It is said that "there is joy in the presence of the angels of God over one sinner that repenteth;" and think you not that it affords God the sincerest joy to be able to forgive the wretched sinner, and save him from the doom of hell? He has no pleasure in our death.

It is a grief to Him to be obliged to execute His law on sinners; and no doubt it affords Him infinitely higher pleasure to forgive us, than it does us to be forgiven. He knows full well what are the unutterable horrors of hell and damnation. He knows the sinner cannot bear it. He says, "Can thine heart endure, and can thine hands be strong in the day that I shall deal with thee? And what wilt thou do when I shall punish thee?" Our Advocate knows that to punish the sinner is that in which God has no delight – that He will forgive and sign the pardon with all His heart.

And think you such an appeal to the heart of God, to His merciful disposition, will have no avail? It is said of Christ, our Advocate, that "for the joy set before Him, He endured the cross, and despised the shame." So great was the love of our Advocate for us that He regarded it a pleasure and a joy so great to save us from hell, that He counted the shame and agony of the cross as a mere trifle. He despised them.

This, then, is a disclosure of the heart of our Advocate. And how surely may He assume that it will afford God the sincerest joy, eternal joy, to be able honorably to seal to us a pardon.

12. He may urge the glory that will redound to the Son of God, for the part that He has taken in this work.

Will it not be eternally honorable in the Son to have advocated the cause of sinners? to have undertaken at so great expense to Himself a cause so desperate? and to have carried it through at the expense of such agony and blood?

Will not the universe of creatures forever wonder and adore, as they see this Advocate surrounded with the innumerable throng of souls, for whom His advocacy has prevailed?

13. Our Advocate may plead the gratitude of the redeemed, and the profound thanks and praise of all good beings.

Think you not that the whole family of virtuous beings will forever feel obliged for the intervention of Christ as out Advocate, and for the mercy, forbearance, and love that has saved our race?

REMARKS

You see what it is to become a Christian. It is to employ Christ as your Advocate, by committing your cause entirely to Him. You cannot be saved by your works, you cannot be saved by your sufferings, by your prayers in any way except by the intervention of this Advocate. "He ever lives to make intercession for you."

He proposes to undertake your cause; and to be a Christian is to at once surrender your whole cause, your whole life and being to Him as your Advocate.

2. He is an Advocate that loses no causes. Every cause committed to Him, and continued in His hands, is infallibly gained. His advocacy is all-prevalent. God has appointed Him as an Advocate; and wherever He appears in behalf of any sinner who has committed his cause to Him one word of His is sure to prevail. Hence you see,

3. The safety of believers. Christ is always at His post, ever ready to attend to all the concerns of those who have made Him their Advocate. He is able to save unto the uttermost all that come unto God by Him; and abiding in Him you are forever safe.

4. You see the position of unbelievers. You have no advocate. God has appointed an Advocate; but you reject Him. You think to get along without. Perhaps some of you think you will be punished for your sins, and not ask forgiveness. Others of you may think you will approach in your own name; and, without any atonement, or without any advocate, you will plead your own cause. But God will not suffer it. He has appointed an Advocate to act in your behalf, and unless you approach through Him, God will not hear you.

Out of Christ, He is to you a consuming fire. When the judgement shall set, and you appear in your own name, you will surely appear unsanctified and unsaved. You will not be able to lift up your head, and you will be ashamed to look in the face of the Advocate, who will then sit both as judge, and Advocate.

5. I ask, Have you retained Him? Have you, by your own consent, made Him your Advocate?

It is not enough that God should have appointed Him to act in this relation.

He cannot act for you in this relation unless you individually commit yourself and your case to His advocacy.

This is done, as I have said, by confiding or committing the whole question of your salvation to Him.

6. Do any of you say that you are unable to employ Him? But remember, the fee which He requires of you, is your heart. You have a heart. It is not money, but your heart that He seeks.

The poor, then, may employ Him as well as the rich; the children, who have not a penny of their own, as well as their rich parents. All may employ Him, for all have hearts.

7. He tenders His services gratuitously to all, requiring nothing of them but confidence, gratitude, love, obedience. This the poor and the rich alike must render; this they are alike able to render.

8. Can any of you do without Him? Have you ever considered how it will be with you? But the question comes now to this – Will you consent to give up your sins, and trust your souls to the advocacy of Christ? to give Him the fee that He asks – your heart, your confidence, your grateful love, your obedience?

Shall He be your Advocate or shall He not? Suppose He stood before you, as I do, and in His hand the book of life with a pen dipped in the very light of heaven, and should ask, "Who of you will now consent to make Me your Advocate?" Suppose He should inquire of you, sinner, "Can I be of any service to you? Can I do anything for you, dying sinner? Can I befriend and help you in any wise? Can I speak a good word for you? Can I interpose My blood, My death, My life, My advocacy, to save you from the depths of hell? And will you consent? Shall I take down your name? Shall I write it in the book of life? Shall it today be told in heaven that you are saved? And may I report that you have committed your cause to Me, and thus give joy in heaven? Or will you reject Me, stand upon your own defense, and attempt to carry your cause through at the solemn judgement?"

Sinner, I warn you in the name of Christ not now to say me nay.

Consent now and here, and let it be written in heaven.

9. Have any of you made His advocacy sure by committing all to Him? If you have, He has attended to your cause, because He has secured your pardon; and the evidence you have in your peace of mind. Has He

attended to your cause? Have you the inward sense of reconciliation, the inward witness that you believe that you are forgiven, that you are accepted, that Christ has undertaken for you, and that He has already prevailed and secured for you pardon, and given in your own soul the peace of God that passeth understanding to rule in your heart? It is a striking fact in Christian experience, that whenever we really commit our cause to Jesus, He without delay secures our pardon, and in the inward peace that follows, gives us the assurance of our acceptance, that He has interposed His blood, that His blood is accepted for us, that His advocacy has prevailed, and that we are saved.

Do not stop short of this; for if your peace is truly made with God — if you are in fact forgiven — the sting of remorse is gone; there is no longer any chafing or any irritation between your spirit and the Spirit of God; the sense of condemnation and remorse has given place to the spirit of Gospel liberty, peace, and love.

The stony heart is gone; the heart of flesh has taken its place; the dry sensibility is melted, and peace flows like a river. Have you this? Is this a matter of consciousness with you?

If so, then leave your cause, by a continual committal of it, to the advocacy of Christ; abide in Him, and let Him abide in you, and you are safe as the surroundings of Almighty arms can make you.

Christ *the* Husband *of the* Church

Wherefore, my brethren, ye also are become dead to the law by
the body of Christ; that ye should be married to another, even to
him who is raised from the dead, that we should bring forth fruit
unto God.[2]

In the discussion of this subject, the following is the order in which
I shall direct your thoughts:

I. Show that the marriage state is abundantly set forth in the Bible,
as describing the relation between Christ and the church.

II. Show what is implied in this relation.

III. The reason for the existence of this relation.

IV. Show the great guilt of the church, in conducting towards Christ
as she does.

V. The forbearance of Christ towards the church.

I. I am to show that the marriage state is abundantly set forth in the Bible,
as describing the relation between Christ and the church.

Christ is often spoken of as the husband of the church. "Thy Maker
is thy husband; the Lord of Hosts is his name." "Turn, O backsliding
children, saith the Lord, for I am married unto you." The church is
spoken of as the bride, the Lamb's wife. "The Spirit and the Bride say,
Come." That is, Christ and the church say, "Come." In 2 Cor. xi. 2, the
apostle Paul says, "For I am jealous over you with godly jealously: for I
have espoused you to one husband, that I may present you as a chaste
virgin to Christ." I can merely refer to these passages. You that are
acquainted with your Bibles, will not need that I should take up time to
show that this relation is often adverted to in the Bible, in a great variety
of forms.

---

[2] *Romans, vii 4.*

II. I am to show what is implied in this relation.

1. The wife gives up her own name, and assumes that of her husband.

This is universally true in the marriage state. And the church assumes the name of Christ, and when united with him is baptized into his name.

2. The wife's separate interest is merged in that of her husband.

A married woman has no separate interest, and no right to have any. So the church has no right to have a separate interest from the Lord Jesus Christ. If a wife has property, it goes to her husband. If it is real estate, the life interest passes to him, and if it is personal estate, the whole merges in him.

The reputation of the wife is wholly united to that of her husband, so that his reputation is hers, and her reputation is his. What affects her character, affects his; and what affects his character, affects hers. Their reputation is one, their interests are one. So, with the church, whatever concerns the church is just as much the interest of Christ, as if it was personally his own matter. As the husband of the church, he is just as much pledged to do everything that is needful to promote the interest of the church, as the husband is pledged to promote the welfare of his wife. As a faithful husband gives up his time, his labor, his talents, to promote the interest and happiness of his wife; so, Jesus Christ gives himself up to promote the welfare of his church. He is as jealous of the reputation of his church, as ever a husband was of the reputation of his wife. Never was a human being so pledged, so devoted to the interest of his wife, or felt so keenly an injury, as Jesus Christ feels when his church has her reputation or her feelings injured. He declares that it were better a man had a mill-stone hanged about his neck, and he were cast into the depths of the sea, than that he should offend one of these little ones that believe in him.

3. The relation between husband and wife is such, that if anything is the matter with one, the other is full of sympathy.

So, Christ feels for all the sufferings of the church, and the church feels for all the sufferings of Christ. When a believer has any realizing view of the sufferings of Christ, there is nothing in the universe so affects and dissolves the mind with sorrow. Never did a wife feel such distress, such broken-hearted grief, if she has occasioned suffering or death to her husband, as the Christian feels when he views his sins as the occasion of the death of Jesus Christ. Let me ask some of these married women present, how you would feel, if your husband, to redeem you from merited ignominy and death, had volunteered the greatest suffering and pain, and even death for you? When you saw his face, how would it affect you? To be reminded of it by any circumstance, how would it melt you down in broken-hearted grief? Now, have you never understood that your sins caused the death of Christ, and that he died for you just as absolutely, as if you had been the only sinner in all God's world? He suffered pain and contempt and death for you. He loved his church and gave himself for it. It is called the church of God, which he purchased with his own blood.

4. The wife pledges herself to yield her will to the will of her husband, and to yield obedience to his will.

She has no separate interest, and ought to have no separate will. The Bible enjoins this and makes it a Christian duty for the wife to conform in all things to the will of her husband. The will of the husband becomes to the faithful wife the mainspring of her activity. Her entire life is only carrying out the will of her husband. The relation of the church to Christ is precisely the same. The church is governed by Christ's will. When believers exercise faith, they are so, absolutely, and the will of Christ becomes the moving cause of all their conduct.

5. The wife recognizes her husband as her head.

The Bible declares that he is so. In like manner, as from the head proceed those influences that govern the body, so from Christ proceed those influences that govern the church.

6. The wife looks to her husband as her support, her protector and her guide.

Every believer places himself as absolutely under the protection of Christ, as a married woman is under the protection of her husband. The woman naturally looks to her husband to preserve her from injury, from insult, and from want. She hangs her happiness on him and expects he will protect her; and he is bound to do it.

So, Christ is pledged to protect his church from every foe. How often have the powers of hell tried to put down the church, but her husband has never abandoned her. No weapon formed against the church has ever been allowed to prosper, or ever shall. Never will the Lord Jesus Christ so far forget his relation to the church, as to have his bride unprotected.

No. Let all earth and all hell conspire against the church, and just as certain as Christ has power to do it, his church is safe. And every individual believer is just as safe, as if he were the only believer on earth, and has Christ as truly pledged for his preservation. The devil can no more put down a single believer, to final destruction, than he can put down God Almighty. He may murder them, but that is no injury. Overcoming a believer by taking his life, affords Satan no triumph. He put Christ to death, but what did he gain by it? The grave had no power over him, to retain him. So with a believer; neither the grave nor hell has any more power to injure one of Christ's little ones, that believe in him, than they have to injure Christ himself. He says, "Because I live, ye shall live also." And, "He that believeth in me, though he were dead, yet shall he live; and whosoever liveth, and believeth in me, shall never die."– There is no power in the universe, that can prevail against a single believer, to destroy him. Jesus Christ is the Head of the church, and Head over all things to the church, and the church is safe.

7. The legal existence of the wife is so merged in that of her husband, that she is not known in law as a separate person.

If any actions or civil liability come against the wife, the husband is responsible. If the wife has committed a trespass, the husband is answerable. It is his business to guide and govern her, and her business to obey; and if he does not restrain her from breaking the laws, he is responsible. And if the wife does not obey her husband, she has it in her power to bring him into great trouble, disgrace, and expense. In like manner, Jesus Christ is Lord over his church, and if he does not actually restrain his church from sin, he has it to answer for, and is brought into great trouble and reproach by the misconduct of his people. By human laws, the husband is not liable for capital crimes committed by the wife, but the law so far recognizes her separate existence, as to punish her. But Christ has assumed the responsibility for his church, of all her conduct. He took the place of his people, when they were convicted of capital crimes, and sentenced to eternal damnation. This is answering in good earnest. And now it is his business to take care of the church, and control her, and keep her from sin; and for every sin of every member, Jesus Christ is responsible, and must answer. And he does answer for them. He has made an atonement to cover all this, and ever liveth to make intercession for his people. So that he holds himself responsible before

19

God for all the conduct of his church. Every believer is so a part of Jesus Christ, and so perfectly united to him, that whatever any of them may be guilty of, Jesus Christ takes upon himself to answer for. This is abundantly taught in the Bible.

What an amazing relation! Christ has here assumed the responsibility, not only for the civil conduct of his church, but even for the capital crime of rebellion against God. There is a sense, therefore, in which the church is lost in Christ, and has no separate existence known in law. God has so given up the church to Christ, by the covenant of grace, that strictly speaking, the church is not known in law. I do not mean that crimes, committed by believers against the moral law, are not sin, but that the law cannot get hold of them, for condemnation. There is now no condemnation to them that are in Christ Jesus. The penalty of the law is forever remitted. The crimes of the believer are not taken into account so as to bring him under condemnation; no, in no case whatever. Whatever is to be done falls upon Christ. He has assumed the responsibility of bringing them off from under the power of sin, as well as from under the law, and stands pledged to give them all the assistance they need to gain a complete victory.

III. I am to explain the reason why this relation is constituted between Christ and his church.

1. The first reason is assigned in the text, "that we should bring forth fruit unto God." A principal design of the institution of marriage is the propagation of the species. So it is in regard to the church. Through the instrumentality of the church, children are to be born to Christ, and he is to see his seed, and to see of the travail of his soul, and be satisfied, by converts multiplied as the drops of morning dew. It is not only through the travail of the Redeemer's soul, but through the travail of the church, that believers are born unto Jesus Christ. As soon as Zion travailed, she brought forth children.

2. Another object of the marriage institution is the protection and support of those who are naturally helpless and dependent. If the law of power prevailed in society, everybody knows that females, being the weaker sex, would be universally enslaved. And the design of the institution of marriage is to secure protection and support to those who are so much more frail, that by the law of force they would be continually

enslaved. So Jesus Christ upholds his church, and affords her all the protection against her enemies, and all the powers of hell, that she needs.

3. The mutual happiness of the parties is another end of the marriage institution.

The same is true of the relation between Christ and his church. Perhaps you will think it strange, if I tell you that the happiness of Christ is increased by the love of the church. But what does the Bible say? "Who, for the joy set before him, endured the cross, despising the shame." What was the joy set before him, if the love of the church was not a part of it? It would be very strange to hear of a husband contributing to the happiness of his wife, that should not enjoy it himself. Jesus Christ enjoys the happiness of his church as much more, as he loves his church better than any husbands love their wives.

4. The alleviation of mutual sufferings and sorrows is one end of marriage.

Sharing each other's sorrow is a great alleviation. Who does not know this? In like manner do Christ and his church share each other's sorrows. The apostle Paul says he was always bearing about in his body the dying of the Lord Jesus; "For as the sufferings of Christ abound in us, so our consolation also aboundeth by Christ." And he declared that one end of all his toils and self-denials was that he might know the fellowship of Christ's sufferings." And he rejoiced in all his sufferings, that he might fill up that which was behind of the afflictions of Christ. The church feels, keenly, every reproach cast upon Christ, and Christ feels keenly every injury inflicted on the church.

5. The principal reason for this union of Christ with his church, is that he may sanctify the church.

Read what is said in Ephesians, v. 22-27. "Wives, submit yourselves unto your own husbands, as unto the Lord. For the husband is the head of the wife, even as Christ is the head of the church; and he is the Savior of the body. Therefore, as the church is subject unto Christ, so let the wives be to their own husbands in everything. Husbands, love your wives, even as Christ also loved the church, and gave himself for it; that he might sanctify and cleanse it with the washing of water by the word. That he might present it to himself a glorious church, not having spot or wrinkle, or any such thing; but that it should be holy and without blemish."

Here then is set forth the great design of Christ in marrying the church. It is that he might sanctify it, and cleanse it, or that it should be perfectly holy and without blemish. John in the Revelation informs us that he saw those who had washed their robes and made them white in the blood of the Lamb. See how beautifully the Bride, the Lamb's wife, is described in the 21st chapter, coming down from God out of heaven, prepared as a bride adorned for her husband.

IV. I will make a few remarks on the wickedness of the church, in conducting towards Christ as she does.

1. Vast multitudes of those who profess to be a part of the church, the bride of Christ, really set up a separate interest.

They have pretended to merge their self-interest in the interest of Christ, but manifestly keep up a separate interest. And if you attempt to make them act on the principle that they have no separate interest, they will plainly show, that they have no such design. What would you think of a wife, keeping up a separate interest from her husband? You would say it was plain that she did not love her husband, as she ought.

2. The church is not satisfied with Christ's love.

Everybody knows what an abominable thing it is for a wife, not to be satisfied with the love of her husband, but continually seeking other lovers, and always associating with other men. Yet, how plain it is that the church is not satisfied with the love of Christ, but is always seeking after other lovers. What are we to think of those members of the church, who are not satisfied with the love of Christ for happiness, but must have the riches and pleasures and honors of the world to make them happy?

Still more horrible would be the conduct of a wife, who should select her lovers from the enemies of her husband, and should bring them home with her, and make them her chosen friends. Yet how many who profess to belong to Christ go away, and give their affections to Christ's enemies. Some will even marry those whom they know to be haters of God and religion. Horrible! Is that the way a bride should do?

3. Everyone knows that it is a disgraceful thing for the wife to play the harlot.

Yet God often speaks of his church as going astray and committing spiritual whoredom. And it is true. He does not make this charge, as a man makes it against his wife, when he is determined to leave her and cast her off. But he makes it with grief and tenderness, and accompanies it with the moving expostulations, and the most melting entreaties that she would return.

4. What would you think of a married woman, who should expect, at the very time of her marriage, that she should get tired of her husband, and leave him and play the harlot?

Yet, how many there are, professors of religion, who when they made a profession had no more expectation of living without sin, than they expected to have wings and fly. They have come into his house, and pledged themselves to live entirely for him, and married him in this public manner, covenanting to forsake all sin, and to live alone for Christ, and be satisfied with his love, and have no other lovers; and yet all the while they are doing it, they expect in their minds that they shall scatter their ways to strangers upon every high hill, and commit sin and dishonor Christ.

5. What are we to think of a woman, who at the very time of her marriage, expected to continue in her course of adultery as long as she lives, in spite of all the commands and expostulations of her husband?

Then what are we to think of professors of religion, who deliberately expect to commit spiritual adultery, and continue in it as long as they live?

6. But the most abominable part of such a wife's wickedness is, when she turns round and charges the blame of her conduct upon her faithful husband.

Now the church does this. Notwithstanding Christ has done all that he could do, short of absolute force, to keep his church from sinning, yet the church charges her sin upon him, as if he had laid her under an absolute necessity of sinning, by not making any adequate provision for preserving his people against temptation. And they are horrified now at the very name of Christian Perfection, as if it was really dishonoring Christ to believe that he is able to keep his people from committing sin and falling into the snare of the devil. And so it has been, for hundreds of years, that with the greater part of the church it has not been orthodox to teach that Jesus Christ really has made such provision that his people may live free from sin. And it is really considered a wonder, that anybody should teach that the bride of the Lord Jesus Christ is expected to do as she pretends to do. Has he married a bride, and made no provision adequate to protect her against the arts and seductions of the devil? Well done! That must be the ridicule of hell.

7. Suppose a wife should refuse to obey her husband and then make him responsible for her conduct.

Yet the church refuses to obey Jesus Christ, and then makes him answer for her sins. This is the great difficulty with the church, that she is continually bringing in her Head for her delinquencies.

8. The church is continually dishonoring Christ.

The reputation of husband and wife is one. Whatever dishonors one, dishonors the other. Now, the church, instead of avoiding every appearance of evil, is continually causing the enemies of God to blaspheme by her conduct.

V. I will say a few words on the forbearance of Christ towards the church.

What other husband, in such circumstances, would suffer the connection to remain, and bear what Christ bears? Yet he still offers to be reconciled, and lays himself out to regain the affections of his bride. Sometimes a husband really loses his affection towards his wife, and treats her so like a brute that, although she once loved him, she loves him no more. But where can anything be found in the character and conduct of Christ, to justify the treatment he receives? He has laid himself out to the utmost, to engross the affections of the church. What could he have done more? Where can any fault or any deficiency be found in him. And even after all that the church has done against him, What is he doing now? Suppose a husband should for years follow his wandering, guilty wife, from city to city, beseeching and entreating her, with tears, to return to his house and be reconciled; and after all, she should persist in going after her lovers, and yet he continues to cry after her and beg her to come back and live with him, and he will forgive and love her still. Is there any such forbearance and condescension known among men?

REMARKS

I. Christians ought to understand the bearing of their sins.

Your sins dishonor Christ, and grieve Christ, and injure Christ, and then you make Christ responsible for them. You sustain such a relation to him, and you ought to know what is the effect of your sin. How does a wife feel, when she has disgraced her husband? How blushes cover her face, and tears fill her eyes! When her guilty offended husband comes into her presence, how she falls down at his feet, with a full heart, and confesses her fault, and pours her penitential tears into his bosom. She is grieved and humbled, and though she loves him, his very presence is a grief, until she breaks down before him, and feels that he has forgiven her.

Now how can a Christian fail to recognise this; and when he is betrayed into sin and has injured Christ, how can he sleep? How can you help realizing that your sins take hold of Jesus Christ, and injure him, in all these tender relations?

II. One great difficulty of Christians is their expecting to live in sin, and this expectation insures their continuance in sin.

If an individual expects to live in sin, he in fact means to live in sin, and of course he will live in sin. It is very much to be feared, that many professors of religion never really meant to live without sin. The apostle insists that believers should reckon themselves dead to sin, that they should henceforth have no more to do with it than if they were dead, and no more expect to sin than a dead man should expect to walk. They should throw themselves upon Christ, and receive him in all his relations, and expect to be preserved and sanctified and saved by him. If they would do this, do you not suppose they would be kept from sin? Just as certainly as they believe in Christ for it. To believe in Christ that he will keep them, insures the result that he will. And the reason why they do not receive preserving grace at all times, as they need and all they need, is that they do not expect it, and do not trust in Christ to preserve them in perfect love. The man tries to preserve himself. Instead of throwing himself upon Christ, he throws himself upon his own resources, and then in his weakness expects to sin, and of course he does sin. If he knew his own entire emptiness, and would throw himself upon Christ as absolutely, and rest on Christ as confidently, for sanctification, as for justification, the one is just as certain as the other.

No one that trusted in God for anything he has promised, ever failed to receive according to his faith, the very thing for which he trusted. If you trust in God for what he has not promised, that is tempting God. If Peter had not been called by Christ to come to him on the water, it would have been tempting God for him to get down out of the ship into the water, and he would have lost his life for his presumption and folly. But as soon as Christ told him to come, it was merely an act of sound and rational faith for him to do it. It was a pledge on the part of Christ, that he should be sustained; and so he was sustained, as long as he had faith. Now, if the Bible has promised that those who receive Christ as their sanctification shall be sanctified, then you who believe in him for this end have just as much reason to expect it, as Peter had to expect he should walk on the waves. It is true, we do not expect a miracle to be wrought to sustain the believer, as it was to sustain Peter. But it is promised that he shall be sustained, and if miracles were necessary, no doubt they would be performed, for God would move the universe, and turn the course of nature upside down, sooner than one of his promises should fail, to them that put their trust in him. If God is pledged to anything, a person that venture(s), on that pledge will find it redeemed, just as certainly as God possesses almighty power. Has God promised sanctification to them that trust him for it? If he has not, then to go to him in faith for preservation from temptation and sin is tempting God. It is fanaticism. If God has left us to the dire necessity of getting along with our own watchfulness and our own firmness and strength, we must submit to it, and do the best we can. But if he has made any promises, he will redeem them to the uttermost, though all earth and all hell should oppose. And so it is in regard to the mistakes and errors which Christians fall into. If there is no promise that they shall be guided just so far as they need, and led into the truth, and in the way of duty and of peace; then for a Christian to look to God for knowledge, and wisdom, and guidance, and direction, without any promises, is tempting God. But if there are promises on this subject, depend on it, they will be fulfilled to the very last mite to the believer who trusts in them; and exercising confidence in such promises is only a sober and rational faith in the word of God.

I believe the great difficulty of the church on the subject of Christian perfection lies here, that she has not fully understood how the Lord Jesus Christ is wholly pledged in all these relations, and that the church has just as much reason and is just as much bound to trust in him for sanctification as for justification. What saith the scripture? "Who of God is made unto us Wisdom, and Righteousness, and Sanctification, and Redemption." How came the idea to be taken up in the church, that Jesus Christ is our Redemption, and has made himself responsible for the meanest individual who throws himself on him for justification shall infallibly obtain it? This has been universally admitted in the church, in all ages. But it is no more plainly or more abundantly taught, than it is, that Jesus Christ is promised and pledged for Wisdom and for Sanctification to all that receive him in these relations. Has he promised that if any man lack wisdom, he may ask of God, and if he asks in faith, God will give it to him? What then? – Is there then no such thing as being preserved by Christ from falling into this and that delusion and error? God has made this broad promise, and Christ is as much pledged for our wisdom and our sanctification, if we only trust in him, as he is for our justification. If the church would only renounce any expectation from herself, and die as absolutely to her own wisdom and strength, as she does to her own righteousness, or the expectation of being saved by her own works, Jesus Christ is as much pledged for one as for the other. The only reason why the church does not realize the same results, is that Christ is trusted for justification, and as for wisdom and sanctification he is not trusted.

The truth is, the great body of believers, having begun in the Spirit, are now trying to be made perfect by the flesh. We have thrown ourselves on Christ for justification, and then have been attempting to sanctify ourselves. If it is true, as the apostle affirms, that Christ is to the church both wisdom and sanctification, what excuse have Christians for not being sanctified?

III. If individuals do not as much expect to live without sin against Christ, as they expect to live without open sins against men, such as murder or adultery, it must be for one of three reasons:

1. Either we love our fellow men better than we do Christ, and so are less willing to do them an injury.

2. Or we are restrained by a regard to our own reputation; and this proves that we love reputation more than Christ.

3. Or we think we can preserve ourselves better from these disgraceful crimes than we can from less heinous sins.

Suppose I was to ask any of you, if you expect to commit murder, or adultery? Horrible! you say. But why not? Are you so virtuous that you can resist any temptation which the devil can offer? If you say so, you do not know yourself. If you have real power to keep yourself, so as to abstain from openly disgraceful sins, in your own strength, you have power to abstain from all sins. But if your only reliance is on Jesus Christ to keep you from committing murder and adultery, how is it, that you should get the idea, that he is not equally able to keep you from all sin? O, if believers would only throw themselves wholly on Christ, and make him responsible, by placing themselves entirely at his control, they would know his power to save, and would live without sin.

IV. What a horrible reproach is the church to Jesus Christ.

V. You see why it is that converts are what they are.

Degenerate plants of a strange vine, sure enough! The church is in such a state, that it is no wonder those who are brought in, with few exceptions, prove a disgrace to religion. How can it be otherwise? How can the church, living in such a manner, bring forth offspring that shall do honor to Christ? The church does not, and individual believers do not, in general, receive Christ in all his offices, as he is offered in the Bible. If they did, it would be impossible they should live like such loathsome harlots.

All Things *for* Good *to*
Those *that* Love God

*"For we know that all things work together
for good to them that love God."*[3]

In illustrating the subject presented in these words, I shall,

I. Show What *the* Passage Means.
II. Illustrate *the* Manner *in* Which This Is Accomplished.
III. Notice Some Particulars *as* Illustrations *of* This Truth.
IV. Show How We Know This Truth, As *the* Text Affirms That We Do.

I. The most important question pertaining to our first topic of remark is, Does the text affirm a universal proposition?

1. The language of the text is universal. It affirms in an unqualified manner that all things work together for good to God's friends. Now it is a good rule of interpretation to understand scripture as it reads, that is, according to its most obvious sense, unless the nature of the affirmation, or some circumstances pertaining to it seem urgently to demand a modification of this meaning. All sound-minded men follow this rule in interpreting both the Bible and all other books and documents.

2. There is nothing in the nature of the case to limit the meaning of this language. On this point especially, there is ample room to enlarge very greatly – but my time will not permit.

3. There is nothing in the context which demands any limitation, but much on the contrary which favors the universal construction.

4. There is nothing anywhere in scripture that conflicts with this, understood as a universal truth. On the contrary the Bible throughout teaches us that everything in the whole plan of God's universal government conspires to this result. All is adapted to befriend his people and to promote their highest good. God is evermore controlling all things for the good of his children. He is their great and good Father.

---

[3] *Rom. 8:28 -*

II. The manner in which this result is accomplished.

This point deserves special consideration, because there are many things, affecting true Christians, which in their present operation seem to work together for their evil and not for their good.

It would require many sermons to investigate this subject thoroughly. At present I can only sketch a few leading principles.

The highest well-being of moral agents depends upon their holiness. This is perfectly obvious. Their holiness, moreover, is conditionated upon knowledge. There can be no holiness in intelligent being without knowledge, and holiness can advance only as knowledge advances. In fact, holiness is nothing else but conformity of heart to knowledge, so that of course there must be knowledge or there could not be holiness. Hence knowledge is both the condition and measure of holiness.

Consequently everything that is a means of knowledge is also a means of holiness. Whatever gives moral agents a knowledge of themselves will if they are holy in character, increase their holiness, for they would cease to be holy if they did not use their knowledge to increase their holiness.

Now all events that occur are providential; that is, they occur under the universal government of God, and occur as they do either because the hand of God controls and shapes them, or because his wisdom permits them to occur as they do, rather than interpose to prevent them. Hence all events reveal God. No event can possibly occur which shall not teach moral agents something concerning God, or themselves, or something useful that they need to know. These events also teach us very much that reveals our relations to God, and hence our duties towards him. And these are precisely the things that are requisite to augment the blessedness of intelligent moral agents.

These remarks apply especially to all those events that fall directly within the range of our present knowledge. But things not within our present knowledge are so related to things that are, as to have a remote bearing upon us, and hence will ultimately come to be known to us. It is probably not too much to presume that all events that ever did or ever shall occur in this world will ultimately be known to all the people of God, and hence will have an important bearing upon their holiness and highest well-being.

III. I am to specify some particulars which serve to illustrate the doctrine of our text.

1. What we call mercies work out the good of those that love God. For if men love God, these mercies quicken their love and gratitude. Every real Christian knows this. It is a precious part of his daily experience.

2. What we call rebukes have also the same tendency to good. Though they may seem evil, yet are they really among the good things that flow to us from the hand of our great Father. They serve to increase our knowledge of God. They show us his faithfulness and assure us that his heart is thoroughly set upon correcting all in us that is wrong – and strengthening all that is right.

The rebukes of God's providence naturally serve to increase our virtue, and hence are often among the very best things God can give us.

3. Again, the crosses of saints work together for their good. Those very things that disappoint their plans, and frustrate their schemes are often among the indispensable things for their real and highest welfare. They are the means by which God breaks them off from their own ways and shows them that they must not have any ways of their own at all. While men are in a state in which they can be crossed, they of course need more discipline. You may recollect the remark made by Dr. Payson that since he had given up his own will and quite lost it so as to have no will of his own, he had not known a single disappointment. He was perfectly satisfied with everything just as God arranged and ordered it, for he had no other will than God's. Now God is seeking to produce such a state of mind in his children that they will say: "I want only to do this or that according to the will of God. Nothing pleases me except what pleases Him. I want to learn His will before I have any special preference of my own. Then if His apparent will changes, I am perfectly pleased, for His will is always best."

Now this state of mind should extend to all events wherein the special will of God is not known by revelation. Hence crosses are exceedingly well calculated for doing good to God's people and are most kindly and wisely designed for this end. We are not to suppose that it is agreeable to our Father to perplex and distress us; but it is agreeable to Him to discipline and chasten us, because he knows that the results are so precious.

It often happens that persons come to see the truth of this in their own case. Then they say, "Now I see how well it has been for me to be disappointed, and how good and wise my Heavenly Father has been in doing it." When I have seen men eagerly set upon some earthly good, I have said to myself: They need to be disappointed, and God will doubtless do it. I shall think it strange if He does not. If they are real Christians and God loves and cares for them as his children, He will surely bring them under discipline to break off their hold upon the world and save their souls.

4. Afflictions should doubtless be accounted among our good things. The Bible teaches this in many passages. One says, "Before I was afflicted I went astray; but now have I kept thy word." Another testifies: "I know that in faithfulness thou hast afflicted me." Afflictions therefore are not to be regarded as evidences of peculiarly great guilt in those who experience them. The case of Job seems to have been designed to teach us this lesson. They rather evince the special faithfulness of God. "Whom the Lord loveth He chasteneth."

5. All those trials which we call temptations are to be accounted among these good things. They very often establish our virtue and greatly develop and strengthen our graces. For this manifestly they were intended. Hence the Apostle says, "My brethren, count it all joy when ye fall into divers[4] temptations; knowing this, that the trying of your faith worketh patience."[5]

6. The responsibilities which God throws upon His children are among the things that work for their good. We may perhaps be made to groan out under these things, and possibly stagger under their burden, yet shall they work out good at last. They are perhaps the very things that are needed to develop our powers. It may be that nothing less than these burdens would make us feel our need of God's daily support, and thus discipline us to daily dependence.

Moreover, some perhaps are naturally so sluggish that God could not save them if He should not lay upon them almost crushing responsibilities.

7. Our own infirmities work out our good. How often do we see this! Physical infirmities and frailties teach us our dependence upon God, and

---

[4] *Various, several -*

[5] *James 1:2, 3 -*

bring us to walk softly with Him and before Him. They often compel us to exercise sobriety, temperance and self-control, and in this way often become our greatest blessings.

Paul had a thorn in the flesh, a messenger of Satan, sent to buffet him. What it was we are not told, but the result plainly shows that it was greatly useful to him.

Now all such things are in certain points of view greatly trying and painful, yet in other respects, they are exceedingly valuable. And when we shall ultimately come to see all their bearings, we shall see that Infinite Wisdom sent them, or at least permitted them, and then overrules them for our good.

8. Our very mistakes often work for our good. Said a pious man once who had fallen into a great error: "Now that is just like me" – that is just like me. I see it now. I might not have seen myself as I am, if that had not happened."

9. The same is doubtless true of the sins of those that love God. Peter's great sin in denying his Lord seems to have been greatly blessed – that is overruled so as to work out good to him. So, with the sins of the children of God generally. Yet they have no excuse for themselves and are none the less guilty for committing them, because God is so good and wise as to counteract some of their evil tendencies and bring good out from them instead of unmingled evil.

10. The infirmities, mistakes and sins of others are among the things that work for our good. Who does not know how much we are benefited by witnessing the sins of others! No thanks indeed to them that their sins are a warning to us, nor can this circumstance lessen their guilt.

Also, the afflictions of others often work out great good to us. The afflictions which we see others suffering may and often do have much the same beneficial result as if we endured them ourselves. So wonderfully has God framed the social economy of our nature and of society.

Finally, it is plain that all events that occur under the providence of God serve to promote the good of His people.

But we must hasten to enquire,

IV. How is it that we know this.

The Apostle says, "We know that all things work together for good to those that love God." Now we cannot suppose he meant to say merely that all inspired men know this. His meaning doubtless is that all Christians may know it. For,

(1.) Reason affirms that it must be so under the government of an infinitely wise and benevolent God. No one can take just views of the character of God without seeing that He must have had a plan for governing this world – must have foreseen all possible and actual results – and must have provided that nothing should occur in vain. That is, He must have determined to prevent the occurrence of all those events which He could not overrule for so much good as on the whole to justify Him in permitting their occurrence. These conclusions are either the direct affirmation of reason, or they are arrived at by the plainest inferences from its intuitions.

(2.) But it is a truth of revelation, and Christians may know it because the Bible teaches it. The Bible everywhere directly or indirectly teaches that God is overruling all events for the good of the righteous.

(3.) Experience and observation universally teach the same thing. Who does not know that all real Christians can say this. Looking over their past history, they can say: "This and that – yea all these things, have been made, through divine mercy and wisdom, to work out my good and fit me for more usefulness here, or, at least for more glory hereafter." It is instructive to see how many of the saints of God can set up here their Ebenezer and testify: "Hitherto has the Lord helped me!"

REMARKS

1. We may blame ourselves for that which upon the whole we do not regret. For example, a man may commit a sin, and of course, he is guilty and inexcusable for this, and ought most surely to blame himself for committing it. His intention is all wrong and he is entirely to blame for it. Yet on the whole it may not be a matter of regret that the sin viewed as an event, occurred, because God has brought a vast amount of good from it.

As a full illustration of this point, take the sin of Satan in tempting Judas and the sin of Judas in yielding to the temptation to betray Christ. This transaction in both Satan and Judas was all evil and nothing else but evil; and was none the less a sin and a great sin because the Lord overruled it for so much good. Yet this good result has been infinitely great. The event therefore is not to be regretted on the whole though Satan and Judas are none the less to be blamed because the wisdom and the love of God have brought so much good from their sins.

You will all recollect the view given in the Bible of the sin of Joseph's brethren in selling him into Egypt. "Be not grieved, said he, nor angry with yourselves that ye sent me hither, for God did send me before you to preserve life." They had sinned, but God had educed so much good from their sinful act, that it was now fit that they should rejoice in those manifestations of wisdom and love.

2. God may blame us and often does, when perhaps on the whole He does not see cause to regret the occurrence of the event. Doubtless God blamed both Judas and Satan, yet He does not regret on the whole that great event towards which their sin directly contributed. Referring to this event, Peter said, "Him, being delivered by the determinate counsel and foreknowledge of God, ye have taken, and with wicked hands have crucified and slain." Their hands were none the less wicked for the good which the Lord brought forth as a result from their evil doing. And it surely may be that the event as a whole even, including the sins of Judas is not regretted by the Most High.

3. It does not follow from this that sin is the necessary means of the greatest good; or that God could not bring about a still greater good if all his creatures were perfectly obedient. It cannot be shown that in every

instance where sin occurs, more good results than would have resulted if holiness had been in its stead. Indeed, we cannot conceive of any higher blessedness to the created universe than universal holiness and its consequent happiness. Now if in every instance when sin occurs, holiness under the same circumstances had occurred, the result would of course be universal holiness, and a degree of blessedness, than which we can conceive of none higher. But it is not my intention now to enter at length into this often disputed subject.

I am aware that those who maintain that sin is the necessary means of the greatest good argue thus; all holiness depends upon knowledge of God; many truths respecting the character of God could never have been revealed if sin had not occurred; hence sin is necessary to the greatest amount of holiness and consequently of real good.

This reasoning would have weight if the case were such that creatures could not be holy without such knowledge of God as nothing can reveal but the occurrence of sin. But none can suppose that such can be the case of moral agents under the government of God. The argument therefore only shows that, sin having occurred, the Lord makes the wisest possible use of it – a fact which none can reasonably doubt. It altogether fails to prove that the state of the universe is better now than it would have been if all had persevered in holiness under the light they had.

But it is especially to my purpose to maintain that God's overruling all things for good to his people forms no apology or excuse for sin. No thanks to the guilty sinner that a God of infinite wisdom can and does manage to work good out of his intended evil. No thanks to him; he is altogether evil and wicked. He does not use it for good himself, nor mean it for good, no more than the devil did in the case of Judas, or than Judas himself did. Suppose that Christ's death, and his death in precisely that manner, was the very best thing that could have occurred; no thanks to Judas or Satan for that; they meant only evil, and all the resulting good must be ascribed to God alone.

Hence it does not follow that we should do evil that good may come. In fact, it is in the nature of the case impossible that a man should do evil for the sake of its resulting good. It is impossible that a man should sin for the sake of doing good thereby, and with this design. Suppose a man to say: let me sin on now for this is the way to do good! Pause a moment and ask: What is sin? Surely it is not doing anything with the design of bringing about good; no but, sin is mere selfishness — is always a trampling down of the greater good for the sake of a far less good for myself. Sin, therefore, never can have the greatest good for its object. Every act that has the greatest good for its design, object or motive, is holiness, not sin.

I am fully aware that the doctrine of my text has been greatly abused. Men have said, "Because sin results in good, therefore let us sin on, and leave it with God to bring out the good which he needs sin in order to educe." — But this is an outrageous perversion of this precious truth. The fact that God can overrule sin for good affords not the least mitigation of the guilt of any sinner. Every sinner is just as guilty as if all sin tended to evil only and as if God had no power or disposition to bring any good out of it whatever.

4. It often happens that we are unable to see how the providence of God will result in our ultimate good. Events that affect us or our friends look utterly dark and we seem almost compelled to say with Jacob, "All these things are against me. All this must be evil to me and mine, and cannot work out my good." But in such cases, we are bound as believing children to dismiss the views which sight gives us, and fall back upon faith. We must now believe God, who says "All things shall work together for good to those that love me." Let all my children believe that and trust their own kind Father!

Now it is not wonderful that in a world like this, framed for a state of trial, events should often assume such an aspect as this. It results in the trial of our faith. And here apply those most pertinent and consoling words of Jesus Christ: "What I do, thou knowest not now, but thou shalt know hereafter." However much, then, the events of divine providence may make us smart, or throw us into perplexity, still let us fall back upon the unfailing promise: "All things shall work together for good to those that love God."

5.* We see why we should give thanks for all things, and why everything that occurs is, in reference to God and His agency in it, a matter of gratitude. We see why we should thank Him for everything he brings about directly by his providence, and also for everything He suffers to be done by moral agents, Himself not preventing them from doing it. We should thank God for not preventing the murderous deeds of Judas and of Satan; for He had wise and good ends in view in not preventing them. Under the circumstances, the Lord did the very best thing he could in permitting those wicked beings to go on, and consummate the murder of his own dear Son.

The same is true of every sin that occurs in the universe. So far as God has anything to do with it, we thank Him, because He does all things well; always doing even in respect to sin the very best thing that under all the circumstances of the case, He can do. For this then, we thank Him. But for what sinners do, we cannot thank them, for they intend only evil. They are to be cursed – not thanked for their sins, and cursed none the less because God always overrules their sin to make it result in just as much incidental good as He can.

6. We see why it is that we are required to rejoice always. Why should not saints rejoice always in all that God is doing? Many of these things, I know, often seem for the present, not joyous but grievous, yet in their remote and ultimate bearings, they always work out great good, and the greatest good which under the circumstances God could effect. A man who is sick may need to resort to many unpleasant medicines; if maimed, he may need for his best good a painful surgical operations; and these things though sad in many of their bearings, are yet good in their ultimate results, and therefore it is cause of gratitude, when they are skillfully and successfully performed. So, with many of the events of life. They come, unmingled with sorrow, but good in their ultimate result, and it would be a great mistake to estimate them only by their present evil, leaving out of view the greater resulting good.

7. It sometimes happens that persons are in this state; "I know," say they, that "all things work together for good to those that love God;" but I am thrown into such circumstances of perplexity and darkness that I cannot tell whether I am one of those who love God or not. The only emotions of which I am sensible are those of pain and agony. I am full of distress, and I can scarcely think of anything else. Especially I cannot feel on any other subjects but my own trials and sufferings.

Now all such persons should look at the attitude of their will and not of their emotions. If they would do so, they would see through this mist, and their perplexities would no longer harass them.

How often have I seen individuals in great distress, under deep trials and perplexities; but strengthening themselves in the Lord their God, they came forth from those scenes of tempest as the sun breaks out from an ocean of storms, all the more glorious for the long and fearful hiding of his beams. So the tried and believing Christian comes forth from his sorest trials, having learned lessons concerning God unknown to him before. Now he sees that his trials are among the greatest blessings he ever received from the Lord.

8. Whatever befalls the saints is to be rejoiced in. Trials may befall our friends, perhaps our own children; but if we have evidence that they love God, we may rejoice in everything that occurs to them. What if afflictions come – wave after wave; all things shall issue in their ultimate good; this is as sure as the word and the government of the eternal God. Even if we should see such a case as that of Job – and none perhaps ever looked more dark – yet even in view of such a case we should rejoice; for we might know that in every similar case as in that, God prepares his afflicted child for a double blessing.

So also, in the trial of Abraham's faith in the matter of offering up Isaac. In this case some things are developed, not often noticed – things pertinent to the case of some Christians at the present day. You recollect, God commanded him to go and take his own son and put him to death, and then offer him as a sacrifice on an altar. What! Abraham might naturally have said, what! God command me to kill my own son? The devil might do this – but how can it be that God should do it? Surely, I never heard anything like this in the ways of God before! This contradicts everything I have ever seen or heard of the Lord Jehovah! He commands me to commit one of the most horrid crimes that ever can be committed. And then this is my son of promise, and God has said that out of him he would make a great nation.

Surely this was one of the most severe trials. It threw Abraham upon his naked faith. He had no resource but to fall back upon simple trust in the Lord, and say, God has spoken – even the wise, the good, the just God, and now let me trust his name! He can raise my Isaac from the dead if need be in order to fulfill his promise.

Thus, he stood his ground, and passed this great and fearful trial. O, how useful and blessed were the results of this trial to Abraham, during all his future life and through all his glorious existence. How gloriously has this example of faith stood out before all the children of God from that day to this! How many have had their faith quickened, directed, edified, by this great example! And perhaps it is not too much to suppose that sooner or later all the angels of heaven will be blessed by the far-reaching influence of this example of trusting and obeying God.

It is a great mistake to overlook these future results of our trials. We ought ever to keep them full in our view. Doing so is indispensable in order to be able to rejoice continually in the Lord, and in all the events that occur under his all-pervading providence. If we fail to do so, how many things will disconcert us and make us stumble to the sore wounding of our peace with God and of our confidence in him.

www.ingramcontent.com/pod-product-compliance
Lightning Source LLC
Chambersburg PA
CBHW020445030426
42337CB00014B/1399

* 9 7 8 1 6 0 3 8 6 7 6 4 1 *